MICRO ENTERPRISE
MARKETING

Micro Enterprise Marketing

How to Start, Promote and Grow Your Micro Business in the Digital Age

SHEILA ATIENZA

Privilege Digital Media

Micro Enterprise Marketing: How to Start, Promote and
Grow Your Micro Business in the Digital Age
Copyright © 2021 by Sheila Atienza

Published by Privilege Digital Media,
Richmond, British Columbia, Canada

This publication is presented to provide integral concepts
and information on the scope covered on the subject matter. Best effort was exerted in order to write the relevant
facts. However, the author and publisher warn the readers
to verify the facts and therefore any changes in those facts
that may take place in the process. In addition, the author
particularly disclaims any liability that is incurred from the
application of the contents of this work. Readers should
consult with an expert to provide advice on their particular situation.

Micro Enterprise Marketing
Privilege Digital Media
Richmond, British Columbia
Canada

PRINT: ISBN: 978-0-9811475-7-4
EBOOK: ISBN: 978-0-9811475-8-1

SUBJECT CATEGORIES:
BUSINESS. ECONOMICS.
  Marketing. General.
BUSINESS. ECONOMICS.
  Small Business.
BUSINESS. ECONOMICS.
  Entrepreneurship.

Contents

Dedication

Dedicated to would-be entrepreneurs
who have confidence in themselves and
take courage and strength to grow

Welcome a New Journey

"Here's a new time;
take a leap,
in your heart believe;
a new journey,
you will plan,
positive outlook you shall welcome."

— Sheila Atienza, Author
Tweets for Your Thoughts

Introduction

Marketing is one of the fundamental components of an enterprise. Some business owners and marketers look at it as the very heart of a business organization, regardless of the size of the enterprise.

An organization may have produced a set of products or services in the world. But without marketing, how can these offerings reach the target customers (or clients) at the right location and at the right time? Without communicating the value or solutions that the business creates, how can the target market discover, learn and understand the benefits of these offerings?

How can you direct all other efforts in your business so that you can reach your goals when there's a missing link?

Marketing supports the overall business strategic goals.

However, marketing for entrepreneurs is somewhat unique in the sense that many micro enterprises have distinct challenges. These challenges are, in most cases, not the kind of problems that worry large-sized organizations.

Many micro enterprises may have, if not, may encounter along the way, these business challenges, such as having limited resources, limited access to funds, and even limited human resources, to carry out other functions in the business.

As an entrepreneur, you perform most of the functions in your enterprise. You are the problem-solver.

You are the one who should actively seek opportunities. You are the one who should exhibit creativity. You are the one who should keep going, despite the challenges that may come your way.

You are the one who should evaluate the overall picture of your micro business. After all, you are the very creator of your micro enterprise.

As an entrepreneur, your venture's success would depend on your entrepreneurial spirit to drive your micro business forward.

This book, **"Micro Enterprise Marketing, How to Start, Promote and Grow Your Micro Business in the Digital Age"**, was created to give new entrepreneurs or would-be entrepreneurs some insights on how marketing can be applied in a micro business setting.

If you're already an entrepreneur but seeking some

information on how to approach your micro enterprise, this book can serve as your reference.

The book explores integral concepts in entrepreneurship. It covers topics that are relevant in the digital age that we are in now.

The book presents content such as new marketing, entrepreneurial marketing, digital marketing, and low-budget marketing.

You will also learn about exploring business growth strategies, creating a strategic plan, and reviewing business growth essentials.

This book, **Micro Enterprise Marketing, How to Start, Promote and Grow Your Micro Business in the Digital Age**, is divided into three parts.

The first part focuses on starting your micro enterprise. The second part covers promoting your micro enterprise. And the third part focuses on growing your micro enterprise. In this book, we use the words 'micro enterprise' (without a hyphen), but you can also refer to it with a hyphen: micro-enterprise.

In **PART 1: HOW TO START YOUR MICRO ENTERPRISE,** we cover the following:

CHAPTER 1 THE ENTREPRENEUR AND ENTREPRENEURIAL MINDSET
The Entrepreneur in You
Entrepreneurial Mindset

CHAPTER 2 HOW TO START YOUR MICRO BUSINESS

From Employment to Self-Employment

Would Your Personality Fit the Role of an Entrepreneur?

What Business Structure Should You Choose for Your Micro Enterprise?

What is Micro Enterprise?

What is Your Business Idea?

The Challenge for Micro Enterprises

In **PART 2: HOW TO PROMOTE YOUR MICRO ENTERPRISE**, we cover the following:

CHAPTER 3 THE NEW MARKETING FOR MICRO ENTERPRISE

How Much Do We Know About Marketing

Keeping Up with Marketing Trends

Entrepreneurs' Digital Knowledge

The Entrepreneur and the Digital Age

CHAPTER 4 ENTREPRENEURIAL MARKETING

The Entrepreneur's Approach to Marketing

Understanding What Entrepreneurial Marketing is

Entrepreneurial Marketing Essentials

CHAPTER 5 DIGITAL MARKETING FOR MICRO ENTERPRISE

Embracing Digital Marketing

Competition and Global Presence

In **PART 3: HOW TO GROW YOUR MICRO ENTER-PRISE**, we cover the following:

1

HOW TO START YOUR MICRO ENTERPRISE

Chapter One

The Entrepreneur and Entrepreneurial Mindset

The Entrepreneur and Entrepreneurial Mindset

CHAPTER 1

The Entrepreneur in You

Entrepreneurial Mindset

The Entrepreneur in You

So, you have decided to enter the wondrous world of entrepreneurship.

The thought of wanting to become an entrepreneur is an admirable thing in itself. It takes some kind of enormous courage to embark upon the route of self-employment.

You must have an idea that you believe can fulfill a specific market need. You are probably excited, and at the same time, exhausted and overwhelmed. Many questions can play in your mind.

There is probably that little voice that keeps bothering you – wanting to find out whether you are making the right decisions or at least making appropriate answers.

Am I taking the right direction?
Is this something that I want to do?
Can this be the start of something great for me?

You may even second-guess yourself.
Am I equipped with the right skills?

You seemed not sure whether you could do it.

And therefore, you may end up asking: *What if I cannot handle the pressure and responsibility of being an entrepreneur?*

* * *

Entrepreneurial Mindset

One of the usual questions entrepreneurs ask in starting a business is finding out whether they have what it takes to succeed in entrepreneurship.

"Do I have the right characteristics of an entrepreneur?"

You could perhaps think of so many familiar words to describe an entrepreneur and entrepreneurship.

Many people would think that a person can achieve entrepreneurial success by having some skills. And these skills may include business skills, technical skills, and probably even more specialized skills.

Indeed, many people would trust that such skills and knowledge would enable an entrepreneur to perform the duties of running an enterprise, and ultimately, lead the business organization with the desired results.

However, despite the acquired skills and knowledge one might have, you might ask, *"How come we see people leaving the business environment they are in, while others are thriving?"*.

What sets an entrepreneurial person apart from the crowd?

While one might think that some business skills may be essential in running an enterprise, a successful entrepreneur must possess some admirable characteristics and abilities that are uniquely theirs, making them stand out from many others. A successful entrepreneur must learn to think beyond ordinary circumstances and approach the entrepreneurial process with creative strategies.

Critical Thinking

The ability to think, find and assess dynamic solutions to business problems - that may arise both in the short-term and the long-term period - should characterize the entrepreneurial mindset of a person.

Beyond technical skills, an entrepreneur must possess the propensity to tackle and solve problems.

Creative Approaches

Entrepreneurship requires creative approaches when facing obstacles and handling problems while at the same time seeing opportunities.

Entrepreneurs are innovative and goal-oriented. They are passionate and determined to achieve their vision. They look at challenges in a positive way. They take on a strategy for their organization with balanced calculated risks.

Entrepreneurial Spirit, Strength and Confidence

Entrepreneurs possess unique strength and confidence that drive others to participate and work on recognized goals.

Now, given these entrepreneurial characteristics, the question to ask, therefore, as a would-be entrepreneur is:

"Am I capable, willing, and ready to take on the challenge?".

Chapter Two

How to Start Your Micro Business

How to Start Your Micro Business

CHAPTER 2

From Employment to Self-Employment

Would Your Personality Fit the Role of an Entrepreneur?

What Business Structure Should You Choose for Your Micro Enterprise?

What is Micro Enterprise?

What is Your Business Idea?

The Challenge for Micro Enterprises

From Employment to Self-Employment

Earning Income from Being Employed to Being Self-Employed

Being Employed

Marketing Yourself Like An Entrepreneur

Why Begin Self-Employment

Freedom in Self-Employment

How Do Self-Employed People Typically Spend their Day?

You Need to Be Available

* * *

Earning Income from Being Employed to Being Self-Employed

How does one even begin with the idea of creating and running a self-employment venture - when you could be quite comfortable with where you are now. Assuming that - you are gainfully employed.

After all, many people have opted to join the employment force in the early part of their career.

Well, that may be because it has always been easier to get started and earn income through employment, right?

Or is it not?

Being Employed

Employment is the most common avenue to earning income in an economy that is thriving.

You just have to submit your resume - begin with a small position in a company, and there you are, you could be rising to the top ranks.

Boom! You would be getting your way to becoming a hard-working member in your workplace. Besides, you have an income that you could receive every month. How could that not be so cool?

Marketing Yourself Like an Entrepreneur

Of course, that would depend on how you market (or promote) yourself in the company.

Did you notice the word "market" (or promote)?

Yes, even when you are a humble, simple, talented employee, you have to market yourself!

You have to think like an entrepreneur. You have to communicate yourself as though you are a most sought-after product. You have to project that you are a unique asset to the company.

You have to think of ways on how you should appear as their ally, that you are the product that can help them solve their problems. "How do I present myself to others, my co-workers, and my bosses in such a way that they will like me?"

Are you assertive enough?

How would they know what you're capable of doing? Or how you could help in the overall goals of the company?

Consequently, you could be earning some reasonable amount of money.

It may not be that substantial at the start, but you could get a promotion in time and receive salary increases.

Why Begin Self-Employment?

So, why bother leaving the employment world and begin self-employment?

The thing with employment is, it could be limiting your potential. Besides, you could also be competing with other workers in your workplace who are eager to achieve a job promotion. And the selection process for candidates for the next position could be overwhelming.

Self-employment could be an option for people who would like to explore their full potential. Self-employed people like the idea of working on flexible hours. Not to mention, they will no longer have to deal with office politics, bossy co-workers, and power-obsessed bosses.

The bottom line is the big word: F-R-E-E-D-O-M.

Freedom in Self-Employment

Being on your own, which means enjoying your freedom and making your decisions, would surround self-employment.

You become your boss.

Who does not like that idea, right? No one would tell you what you should do. No one would bother to correct what you could be doing.

And yes, you have your hours. And you could decide how you would want to spend these precious hours.

But then, when does freedom begin and end in self-employment?

How Do Self-Employed People Typically Spend their Day?

Do you wonder, "How do self-employed people typically spend their day?".

The answer would depend on your business organization, your operation, and your target market.

When do your customers contact you? Would that be 24/7? Would you have a specific schedule? Would you work the typical eight to five? Or nine to six? Or would shifting schedules be possible to operate?

The words: flexibility and freedom are among the common motivational factors for going for self-employment. But self-employed people such as freelancers, creative consultants, and many other entrepreneurs have their respective approaches in managing their time.

You Need to Be Available

We could mostly agree that many self-employed people could enjoy freedom and flexibility. However, the idea remains relative to what self-employed people do.

You must realize that as an entrepreneur, you do not exist all by yourself and for yourself.

Being an entrepreneur or a self-employed person means that you have to connect to your target audience - your customers (or your clients).

You need to be available when they are available or when they expect that you would be there for them.

How do you plan to spend your hours in your business operation?

We go back to the same kind of question again. I know, being on your own, working on your own, could mean deciding on the hours that you want. After all, you decided to go on entrepreneurship with the idea that you have your own time.

But does that mean that being an entrepreneur, you should work anytime and anywhere you want?

Of course, that would depend on the many aspects of your business and the kind of market or customers you serve.

How do you plan to service and communicate with your customers or clients?

Do you have a physical location for your business? Then, you may need to specify your hours of operation. When could customers (or clients) come into your office or location?

If you do business online, you could decide how you would set your restrictions.

When and how could customers contact you? Or when could customers expect to hear back from you?

The point is, you would need to be available at the time when your clients or customers would need to communicate with you or access your products or services.

* * *

Would Your Personality Fit the Role of an Entrepreneur?

An Entrepreneur Wears Many Hats

Knowing Your Customers

No Stopping for the Entrepreneur

How You Fit to Become an Entrepreneur

Entrepreneurship is Not Static

* * *

An Entrepreneur Wears Many Hats

We could all agree that an entrepreneur wears many different hats.

Yes, you are your big boss. But you also assume the roles of managing and maintaining many other aspects in your business - from finance and accounting to marketing and customer service.

Like any person who applies for a job, an entrepreneur must also assess the qualifications for the role of being self-employed. It's like preparing an equivalent resume - or you can call it an entrepreneur's profile. What qualities do you possess? What are your skills? How do you describe yourself? Can you perform the role - or many other roles at that?

You probably did not intend to go for entrepreneurship simply because you got bored, did you?

You are not in the world of entrepreneurship to simply create a business. There are many fundamental reasons.

You are in business to respond to many questions. And these questions, even if you have already answered at some point, will still have to be answered in the present time. And again, in the future, as though you are in a circle. And that circle would keep on rolling.

When you reach a final phase, you could be up for another start. It never stops. And you may wonder - "There's no stopping?".

Knowing Your Customers

Identifying your customers or audience (whom you are targeting to service or offer your solutions) would be the very first of all the aspects of your business with which you deal.

And why is that?

It is because everything else - in your business or marketing mix - would depend on your target market.

Some questions you will have to keep asking yourself can be:

Are my customers satisfied with the services or products that I deliver to solve their problems?

If they are not happy enough, how could I improve on the solutions that I provide?

How do my competitors perform? Are their customers satisfied?

Wait, my competition is doing better. Should I stop already?

No Stopping for the Entrepreneur

As an entrepreneur, there seems to be no stopping. And as we have mentioned, your world full of questions would go on and on. You may reach the full circle. But you may keep rolling. And go back again.

More questions would arise. And some problems could trigger even more stress that could affect your well-being.

So what if you are transitioning from being employed to being an entrepreneur? What should you expect in terms of changes?

You should remind yourself of the many aspects that go with self-employment. Review and reflect upon the topics that we have covered thus far. To you, what does freedom entail?

How You Fit to Become an Entrepreneur

Still, the question, whether you are fit to become an entrepreneur bothers you. You worry, what if - after all the wanting and planning you have been doing to become an entrepreneur - you fail?

How do you keep the drive and desire of entrepreneurship flowing? How do you pick yourself up from being down? How do you keep the enthusiasm in you?

Being enthusiastic and maintaining enthusiasm would depend on the kind of personality you have. What are your tendencies, and how do you manage or control the many aspects of your being?

* * *

Entrepreneurship is Not Static

How Do You Keep Going

The world of entrepreneurship is never static. It keeps evolving. And it could go so fast - given the digital technologies that we could use and experience. We are all connected with these changes. And it will keep happening. So how do you keep up?

It is up to us to find ways to keep learning and being open to possibilities.

Being an entrepreneur is also being resilient.

After a fall, you will have to rise again. You will have to keep going - on and on - in the middle of difficulties - in the world where you are. That means - you will have to maintain the radiance and creativity in you, no matter how big or small the trials you may encounter along the way.

* * *

What Business Structure Should You Choose for Your Micro Enterprise?

Which business structure should you form?

Business Entity Comparison

Sole Proprietorship

Partnership

Corporation

Deciding on Your Business Structure

* * *

You are ready to take your small business to the next level. You have been thinking of whether to take the route of sole proprietorship - or incorporation.

Should you incorporate?

You know, perhaps, of many small businesses or entrepreneurs that start with being sole proprietors.

The operation is simple. You could manage just fine.

Your resources may be limited, but it would seem okay. Sales are coming in nevertheless.

You rely on yourself - doing most of the work, if not all, and you survive just as well.

Entrepreneurs are attracted to the idea of sole proprietorship – and may opt to maintain this way, given its simplicity and straightforward approach.

So why should you consider the idea of incorporation?

What are the benefits of incorporating your business, anyway, right?

As your business grows, your needs and circumstances may change.

And the one approach you got used to applying for your business may no longer be enough to meet your growing needs.

Some business owners would look at the idea of incorporation from the very beginning of establishing the business.

Which business structure should you form?

Have you already thought about the business structure that would work best for your business operation?

It is imperative for small business owners, especially the new entrepreneurs, to understand the pros and cons in pursuing their choice for business structure.

Which one should you choose:
· Sole Proprietorship
· General Partnership
· Corporation

Researching and comparing various business structures can be challenging - and worse, it could be time-consuming.

As an entrepreneur, you must understand, analyze and decide on which business structure would be right for your micro business venture.

More than anything, you will need to think through and review your needs and your future requirements.

Ask yourself - "Which one would help me in achieving my business objectives and goals - both short-term and long-term goals?".

Depending on which country, province or region, you operate your business, you will find that there are different business structures available.

For example, some of the options for USA-based enterprises are:

· Sole Proprietorship
· General Partnership
· Limited Partnership
· Limited Liability Company
· Professional Limited Liability Company
· C-Corporation
· Professional Corporation
· Non-Profit Corporation
· S-Corporation

In Canada, the most typical business structures are sole proprietorship, partnership, and corporation.

Business Entity Comparison

SOLE PROPRIETORSHIP

Sole proprietorship seems the easiest and simplest structure to form. It is uncomplicated for a small business or a micro enterprise. Also, it appears to be less expensive. The application process seems way quicker to accomplish, and therefore, more practical. If you are up for a one-person operation, sole proprietorship seems the path to go.

However, when it comes to liability, the owner personally handles debts and liabilities that may arise in business.

PARTNERSHIP

1.) GENERAL PARTNERSHIP

Forming a partnership, such as a General Partnership, would seem appropriate for some operations. Small business owners will find that this structure is reasonable and can work even for a small enterprise.

One of the advantages of this structure is allowing the general partners to raise funds for their venture.

Also, the process of business formation would be a little less complicated than a corporation.

With General Partnership, the partners are responsible for business debts and liabilities.

2.) LIMITED PARTNERSHIP

Some people may form a business, considering the Limited Partnership structure. They choose this form, especially if they are in the real estate trading or investing business.

As partners deal with real estate transactions, forming and operating this structure requires more funds, and therefore, could be very expensive.

CORPORATION

Corporation seems the most expensive and difficult to create of all the three popular forms of business organization.

With a corporation, business owners need to file formal requirements and reports, as well as maintain status as a corporation.

One of the most recognized advantages, though, for creating a corporation is asset protection.

Also, a business organization under a corporation can have several shareholders. The corporation can raise funds for the business organization in the form of stocks.

With a corporation, business owners can create more opportunities for the business in terms of capitalization.

With proper business leadership, management, and corporate strategies, a corporation can create outstanding growth - depending on the direction it decides to take - considering all other factors that affect its operations.

Deciding on Your Business Structure

The business structure you will choose to establish your micro enterprise would depend on the type of business you have, in which industry you are, and the complexity it entails.

You will have to decide - considering many other aspects that may impact your business venture.

Whatever business structure you decide to form, you will have to deal with its respective advantages and disadvantages.

It is a matter of how you can handle the difficulties. And how you will manage the resources to combat any challenges that come your way.

One reminder, though, it is always good to seek the help of professional consultants and address your situation.

* * *

What is Micro Enterprise?

So how do we define a micro enterprise (or micro-enterprise)?

Others call it Micro Business.

We know that from the word "micro" we actually mean "small". But how small is a micro enterprise or micro business?

From the business perspective, a micro enterprise could refer to a small business with five or fewer employees.

Therefore, we could practically define a micro enterprise, as:

> *"A micro enterprise is a kind of small business venture, with one-to-five employees managed by an entrepreneurial person who, in most cases, is the business owner. A micro enterprise owner (or manager) must think of creative approaches to respond to business unique challenges and threats and find opportunities to succeed and thrive."*

A micro enterprise is a kind of small business venture, with one-to-five employees managed by an entrepreneurial person who, in most cases, is the business owner. A micro enterprise owner (or manager) must think of creative approaches to respond to business unique challenges and threats and find opportunities to succeed and thrive.

**

What is Your Business Idea?

By now, I suppose you have been thinking of forming your organization for your small business venture or micro enterprise.

However, before you could do that, you will have to think of even more important things. What is your business idea? Whom do you want to target to offer your product or service as a solution to the market's unmet needs?

What kind of business do you think would be possible for you, considering your interests and resources?

An entrepreneurial person always has the desire to think of ideas, in which one could wish that one day that business idea could turn into a profitable small business.

Does one need to have an exceptional talent to pursue new concepts or innovation?

Any aspiring entrepreneur can pursue entrepreneurship with unique processes. However, an entrepreneur must have the driving spirit and the enthusiasm to pursue various stages in entrepreneurship.

Entrepreneurs know that they have their capability to create their opportunities and fortunes. They can turn things around and make them happen.

There are many ways in which we could further describe entrepreneurship.

We could say entrepreneurship is a journey. One can get to the destination faster, while others can take their time to perfect their venture.

So what is required to pursue entrepreneurship?

Entrepreneurship requires different approaches in managing an enterprise.

Entrepreneurship requires different approaches in managing an enterprise.

Most of the time, it requires some kind of creativity, and practicality in dealing with problems, while, at the same time, finding opportunities.

What Business To Start

There are instances that you may have available resources, such as financial resources, and you may simply want to research and assess what sort of business you can get in.

You can start with the list that we have here. It can give you some ideas on what business to start and go from there.

Home-Based Food Business,
Catering Service Business,
Handyman Business,
Home Cleaning Business,
Home Daycare Business,
ESL Teaching Business,
Art Teaching Business,
Gift Basket Business,
Landscaping Business,
Trendy Fashion Boutique,
Pet Business,
Creative Services Business,
Internet Research Business.

Of course, there are more ideas out there. Better yet, ask yourself these questions:

What am I good at doing? (Or in some cases, you can ask, *What do I enjoy doing?*)

Is there a market for it?

What opportunity could I see in this industry?

Who are my competitors? How are they doing in terms of demand or sales?

What are my resources?

How would I finance and operate my micro enterprise?

* * *

The Challenge for Micro Enterprises

The challenge for most micro enterprises would be not just how to start the business but how to promote, grow and manage the enterprise so that it becomes sustainable and profitable.

What resources are already available to you as a business owner?

How do you manage the resources that you have?

How do you respond to challenges brought about by the economic crisis?

Would your product fulfill the needs of your target customers or clients?

What makes you and your business unique?

How do you differentiate your offering from other products available in the marketplace?

What are your strengths and weaknesses?

How do you respond to business opportunities and threats?

2

HOW TO PROMOTE YOUR MICRO ENTERPRISE

Chapter Three

The New Marketing for Micro Enterprise

The New Marketing for Micro Enterprise

CHAPTER 3

How Much Do We Know About Marketing

Keeping Up with Marketing Trends

Entrepreneurs' Digital Knowledge

The Entrepreneur and the Digital Age

How Much Do We Know About Marketing?

IF YOU HAVE BEEN DOING MARKETING FOR MANY YEARS

If you've been doing marketing for many years, perhaps you have been a marketing manager of a firm, or a business owner yourself, you may find this question: *"How Much Do We Know About Marketing?"* not that quite thought-provoking.

Well, maybe.

At some point, we know that we have mastered marketing skills long enough - that we can define or explain fully what we understand about marketing.

And this could happen, in a case, when we assume that the company we've been with, all these years, remains in its finest. It is as though there are no challenges whatsoever that could be happening in the business.

We could be complacent and think that change may not be necessary or may not happen soon.

Again, maybe.

If we examine what other marketing experts are saying about marketing, we can learn that there are different approaches and different ways to apply strategies in marketing. Indeed, we will find that there are different definitions of marketing or at least different ways of putting meaning to the word marketing.

The bottom line, marketing is aimed at primarily satisfying the needs of customers. All other parts in the mix must blend to deliver the right solutions to the target market.

That is a given.

However, we must also remember that change is something we cannot avoid in the process. It will happen, whether we like it or not.

Market needs will gradually grow and progress depending on how others are doing.

It's human nature. People socialize and learn from others.

What we find working in the past may not work at the moment. And as market demands increase over time, how prepared are we to respond to such needs?

If we look at some mid-to-large companies that have been successful a decade or two ago, with great start-ups, IPO's, and all, and have attained a significant market position in their industry, how well, do you think, they have consistently delivered? What were they doing to keep up with the pace of change?

We've seen many companies failed. Some have survived. Some companies are performing well and are pleased with their market share. And there are new players. Competitors. Allies or Foes. And they are all doing the function of marketing. And so are the small business owners and entrepreneurs.

So, the question goes back, what is marketing? And yes, how much do we know about marketing?

Emerging trends are apparent. We need to listen to our customers. We need feedback. We need information. We need to keep learning. We need to embrace the word innovation. We may need to change our approach. We need to see what is going on in the digital world. And how well people are embracing the digital life that they live and experience - day in and day out.

Marketing has changed, indeed, in an inconceivable way. Digital trends have tremendously changed the marketing landscape. And if we need to keep our business going and thriving in this era, what do we need to do?

We need to **redefine marketing.**

IF THIS IS YOUR FIRST TIME DOING MARKETING

If this is your first time in marketing, you can keep an open mind. There are many resources available to help you (improve your skills and) respond to the challenges of the evolving world of marketing.

* * *

Keeping Up with Marketing Trends

It is astonishing to see how the world of marketing has evolved to this day. Marketing activities have never been as challenging as today, that we, marketers, should be able to find ways to keep up with the trends. It is not to say, though, that every kind of marketing tool that we see around would be as useful as we hope they all would be. Of course, that would depend on the type of business or product that we have. We, all, could hope that these tools would help us boost our means to communicate effectively with our target audience (our customers).

The point that we need to consider is that it would not harm to see and learn what is out there and try to understand how the new marketing proponents can help us grow.

Every new marketing tool that we come across online could give internet users some kind of value.

Every day, we often discover new websites, which may belong to large corporations, mid-size companies, and even small businesses and entrepreneurs. And if we are to research through our local cities and see the number of companies that enter the business world, it is not surprising to find out how many are, indeed, attracted to get into entrepreneurship.

So how do these entities compete with existing companies or competitors? How do they strengthen their competitive advantage? Or do they even recognize that?

Let us face it not everyone is acquainted with the tools to help them become what they could, potentially, be. Sometimes, we get so busy with day-to-day business activities that we forget to look at how we could effectively gather information. Or how can we, indeed, identify places in which our customers frequent these days. And who influences their decision-making?

Isn't it about time that we pause awhile? And, sincerely, listen to what our customers are, indeed, telling us.

It is no longer enough to solely use traditional marketing or simply employ what used to work. It is not about looking at just the present time. It is about going forward. It is about the future. It is about the stakeholders. It is about the clients. It is about the consumers. It is about the employees. And, of course, it is all about others who can influence the future of your business.

And perhaps, by trying to look at all emerging factors and planning to properly, listen and communicate with our target audience and using the appropriate marketing tools available, only then we would be able to know how we can take the most important steps and be able to keep up with the trends.

That is the beauty of marketing. It is an enormous world. Despite uncertainties, we need to function, not just to keep up with the pace, but to be consistent with, if not discover, what makes us unique in the eyes of our target audience. No matter how big or small we are.

* * *

Entrepreneurs' Digital Knowledge

As an entrepreneur, you know how vital it is to prepare yourself with the necessary tools to arm you as you carry out your plan.

In addition to your business background or work experience, you probably have also attained some kind of knowledge to guide you throughout your marketing adventure. You must be confident with what you have learned. You probably had an exciting opportunity to have applied some knowledge that you have gained. You knew that some things work just right. After all, you made it happen. Perhaps, some five years ago or seven years ago. So, what is it that bothers or worries you?

Do you worry about how to approach your business with the new marketing? Sincerely, ask yourself, "How do I direct my business in the digital space?".

Is your small business online? If you must know,

your competition is. And so are your target customers or clients.

Do you have a website that can help inform or educate your customers? Do you have web content that can guide your customers on how to use your products or services? What makes your business the go-to place so that your customers could keep coming back?

How do you start and continue your conversation with your audience online? Are you able to monitor online reviews on social networking sites? Are you aware of how others view your business? Are you aware of how your customers share their experience, if any, in using your company's products or services?

How do you establish your online reputation?

Considering the growing trend with online marketing, it is but a good idea that entrepreneurs learn the emerging marketing tools. Understand the importance of creating a website for your business. Manage your online content and review your web analytics.

There are, indeed, many things about marketing to learn these days. You must have noticed that the technological tools today are, in many ways, different from the tools used in the past.

Have you observed how computers are turning into different forms? Now, we are using several devices, such as tablets, smartphones, and desktop computers, to manage some work activities.

Don't you think that somehow, it would be a good thing to learn new technologies and applications?

Technological advancement can help us increase our knowledge, enhance our skills, and equip ourselves to better approach our business and life.

Think about your goals.

Think about personal growth.

Think about lifelong learning.

* * *

The Entrepreneur and the Digital Age

We are, undoubtedly, in an era of digital evolution that signals change in how people work and interact with one another. People use technologies not only to find information online but to communicate, connect and collaborate with other people.

It seems to be the path we are all going. Many people have found success in meeting their needs, from buying and selling products to subscribing and paying for services they need. Behaving online can even help establish a reputation that can either promote or harm your image or your brand.

Digital media and technologies are, therefore, not only beneficial to early adopters of technologies but equally important to many people (from different parts of the globe) who use online communication in their daily lives.

It is even astonishing to witness how much people have embraced the use of multiple devices, such as the use of smartphones and tablets. People do not just use one device to get information about anything online. But they could use multiple devices, depending on where they are and when they want.

People need to go wireless. They need to go mobile. They need to be able to access information anytime and anywhere they go.

That can lead us to think and assess how empowering digital technologies can be. Digital media can shape consumers' thinking and behaviour. It allows them to respond or interact in ways that would have been unimaginable some years ago.

Consumers can do so many things online, given access to internet technologies. They can shop online, do mobile banking, browse mobile apps, exchange video chats, play video games, and watch various YouTube videos.

What is even more astounding is that digital evolution and transformation are happening already. You should not miss out on these digital happenings.

As we decide to go digital, we can probably expect more challenges in our marketing activities, considering the competition and the global marketplace.

But, take heart. What could come with these challenges are great possibilities. Let us explore the brighter side.

One thing sure about the emergence of this new media is that it can create opportunities for many of us. Digital technologies can be an ally to entrepreneurs and marketers. Or practically to anyone trying to promote anything, a product, a service, or any idea to anyone.

What marketers should examine, though, is how to use digital media and technologies to work to their advantage. What can digital marketing do to help you prosper in this digital era?

Whether you are starting up a micro enterprise or looking for ways to improve your small business – or trying to keep up with the challenge of the present digital world, you will need to employ digital strategies and channels to complete your marketing mix. That would help your business prosper and thrive in the digital space. You would be able to increase brand awareness and improve relations with your target audience (or customers).

As an aspiring entrepreneur or even as an established small business owner, it is imperative to acknowledge that we are in a digital generation dealing with prospects or customers accustomed to the use of information technology. Customers have embraced the use of digital lingo as they access information online. They are comfortable going mobile, connecting seamlessly with family members or friends, using video communication and various social media tools.

People who thrive digitally tend to appreciate the convenience, cost-effectiveness, and opportunities afforded and delivered electronically.

Many people would search for things online, making Google their leading search engine. Many would express their fondness about anything. Many would share with others their experience – whether positive or disappointing.

It is vital that entrepreneurs become familiar with the digital language their customers are using. The goal is to connect and communicate with the target audience. This will help entrepreneurs understand consumers' needs better. Gone are the days when customers can be content receiving whatever it is that companies or manufacturers produce, giving them limited choices.

Customers now have strongly become and must be the very core of the marketing mix. Many of them share their comments on how well they like the products they've purchased or why they don't like the products they've used. In some way, we can see how good it can be for established business owners and even new entrepreneurs.

Customers are instrumental to how entrepreneurs can improve their products. For that reason, entrepreneurs today could benefit a lot in refining the product or doing innovation. After all, entrepreneurs produce goods or provide services to satisfy the needs of their target market.

Digital media can allow customers to engage with companies and manufacturers and even collaborate with other entities in ways we could never have thought some years ago. Imagine how many individuals today have opened social media accounts or have started blogs. Generally, any individual can begin producing content that is rich with engaging text, pictures, and even videos.

One cannot almost imagine how much content can be produced each day, given the countless number of people getting into the social media networks.

Customers and consumers who go online seek out information. They could browse web pages, read content, and share information.

There seems to be an explosion of content happening today with the so-called user-generated content. Social media networks have become the "in" thing. It has become conventional.

Social media has created new media. The roles have changed in that customers can now assume the task of creating content.

The saying that goes "content is king" still is true. The power that lies behind digital content can seem inconceivable yet, can enormously create a strong mark that can capture the hearts and minds of the audience.

That is the essence of doing marketing in the new age of media.

Chapter Four

Entrepreneurial Marketing

Entrepreneurial Marketing

CHAPTER 4

The Entrepreneur's Approach to Marketing

Understanding What Entrepreneurial Marketing is

Entrepreneurial Marketing Essentials

The Entrepreneur's Approach to Marketing

By now, you must be familiar with the word entrepreneurship. You know that as an entrepreneur, you would probably like to produce or create something - a product that you believe your target customers will buy. Or perhaps, you would like to offer a service that you believe will help your target customers solve their problems. In essence, you are creating your income opportunity. And that is good. And you can be enthusiastic about this newly-found, exciting entrepreneurial journey in your life. You seem to have that idea. You know that you can create your wealth through your vision. And you believe you can accomplish your vision through hard work.

But, how easy or complicated is it to get into the world of entrepreneurship? Yes, it can be exciting. It can drive you. But up to what extent?

The thing is, you may come to a certain point in which you realize that being an entrepreneur is not as easy as becoming an employee. If you have been employed for some years or at some point in your life, you know that by working for someone else (or a company at that), you can expect to receive a salary at a scheduled date. In fact, as a starter or innovator of a product, you probably know that you do not have a set of customers yet who will buy from you at the outset. You know that you will need to build upon a strong customer base that will give you the positive income that you wish to create in the first place.

So, how would you be able to get these customers? How would you be able to reach out to these people?

The idea about entrepreneurship is not exactly something you can compare with creating medium to large-scale businesses (in which you see companies competing or excelling in their respective industries). Of course, we could learn from large companies like Microsoft, Amazon, and Apple. They must have started from being small at some point. We must recognize, however, entrepreneurship comes with its respective challenges. These challenges may not be something that large businesses dwell on. And although having a vision for your venture is a very vital aspect of driving your enterprise to the next possible level, entrepreneurship is looked at as a different category in the way one should manage and grow one's business.

Entrepreneurship poses many unique opportunities as well as several obstacles and challenges. What sets a successful entrepreneur apart from other entrepreneurs is that a successful entrepreneur has the positive mindset to identify opportunities in the middle of seeing, encountering, and experiencing difficulties.

What matters more is having the ability to spot, at the earliest possible opportunity, problems or difficulties that there may be. What sort of approaches are you prepared to undertake, and for how long should you do it? What are your resources? What are your limitations?

The good news, though, is – entrepreneurship has evolved into becoming a separate field (from the traditional business sense) and that it requires a different set of strategies. And therefore, more practical approaches can be applied as new concepts of marketing emerge.

As an entrepreneur, you probably have noticed or might have feared that one of the biggest possible challenges to compete in the marketplace is the presence of the big companies, who seem to have taken the large pie in terms of market share. And therefore, it is inevitable to pose that big 'HOW' question. Yes, how can a micro enterprise compete with the big players?

The field of entrepreneurship requires that a person must have the capability of learning and applying new approaches. That means you recognize great possibilities.

As an entrepreneur, you could learn to be more open and flexible. And isn't that a good thing? You could adapt. And you could be more unconventional.

That's the wonder of marketing. It enables you to create your unique voice. You can highlight your unique presence or brand. Think of all companies that have capitalized on the use of the internet and digital technology.

With the enormous impact of the internet and how people responded to these new technologies, many entrepreneurs and innovators have made it in their respective industries.

And it is not surprising. You will perhaps be able to cite many other product innovators and visionaries. Did we have to mention the names such as Mark Zuckerberg (the founder of Facebook) or Jeff Bezos of Amazon? And do you recognize Lynda Weinman? She was the founder, along with her husband, of an online training site called: Lynda.com. They later sold their business venture to the social network company we know as LinkedIn.

We could hear and even cite many more success stories. The point here is, many successful companies started from being small at some point. And they all have their unique entrepreneurial characteristics.

Marketing is a vital component in an entrepreneurial venture. It is an essential tool available to any enterprise willing to capitalize on it.

Marketing can help shape the identity of an enterprise in the minds of the target consumers.

* * *

Understanding What Entrepreneurial Marketing is

So we've been talking about the idea of entrepreneurial marketing, but you may be wondering, "What is this thing exactly about?".

If we compare the practice of marketing from the traditional marketing sense, you will perhaps notice that large-sized companies tend to move with some kind of formal structure. They strongly depend on market research and statistics. They hold several consultations. They seek approval from the big bosses before they could come up with their decisions.

Big companies need to consider several stakeholders. And that would include their investors, internal people (their employees), and external publics (the consumers, channels, and suppliers).

With micro enterprise marketing, most entrepreneurs or marketing strategists would agree that entrepreneurial marketing thrives through the entrepreneur's marketing spirit and would not focus on just one marketing strategy. Entrepreneurs tend to be more dynamic in their approach. They could experiment and apply several unconventional marketing approaches to help them gain traction in the crowded, competitive, demanding markets.

Entrepreneurs tend to create and evaluate many entrepreneurial marketing strategies. Entrepreneurs would create many of these possible strategies out of the need to create one. They do it in an instance they deem necessary.

Having a micro enterprise entails the need for the business owner to be flexible, motivated, and open-minded. As an entrepreneur, you would be ready to become proactive. You recognize that there is no opportunity for making excuses, for procrastinating and delaying. An entrepreneur is expected to come up with not just one option to deal with a problem but is open and innovative enough to think through many possibilities.

Compared to a large-sized business, a micro enterprise may have limited access to resources, logistics, and manpower.

Despite this reality on limitation, micro enterprises could still perform at their very best.

That is when the idea of creativity would come into the picture. Entrepreneurs can promote their enterprise, given the limited budget. Entrepreneurs can create a combination of promotional strategies to capture the attention of their audience. Entrepreneurs would think of several approaches. And they would do this until they could see that things are working for their enterprise.

Applying effective entrepreneurial marketing takes into consideration several factors, such as risks, control, and innovation.

Effective marketing campaigns can focus on the

value the enterprise could offer to the customers. How unique is the offering? What is the competitive advantage? Why would the customers buy from your enterprise when they could get that from large industry players? Given that scenario, a micro enterprise will need to emphasize its strengths. For example, a micro enterprise can highlight the benefit of its offering (innovative product and approach to personal service). Is there any particular feature in the product that makes it extra special? You can capitalize on that feature by focusing on what it does. Let us say such a feature can add convenience, speed up the process, or even help a user save time and money.

Customers would eventually recognize your brand and your company's presence. And gradually will turn to you and your products because of that promise you created. The process does not end there. You will need to ensure that the product or service is delivered as expected and on time. The key here would be customer satisfaction. And as a micro enterprise, how do you ensure that you can commit to the customer's expectation?

The whole idea of marketing takes a creative process. And being an entrepreneur, a single approach or strategy to a problem may not be enough. You must identify what sorts of problems your clients might have. What seems to be their concerns? What are their worries? How can your offering respond to that particular worry? As an entrepreneur, you will always need to be proactive. And always strive to listen. It is vital to understand and evaluate your customers' needs closely.

As an entrepreneur, you must remember the challenges that come with a newly-established enterprise. An entrepreneur or owner of a newly formed business may need to employ more efforts in marketing. You must realize that taking one promotional stint to introduce your offering or your company to the marketplace would probably be not enough. You will need to increase the frequency of your promotional activities. And you will need to do it consistently.

If you look at large-sized companies (and even the not so large enterprises) on the number of times they promote their product (in some media channels, such as the television), you will have noticed that their TV ads have perhaps been played numerous times in several days, and even weeks. And in the process, you must have memorized the lyrics of the jingle or the dialogue or words used in the advertisement. You would notice that there seems, perhaps, some kind of impact on a consumer that one cannot seem to explain. Yet, there could be a possibility that one might want to try out the product at some point. And that is probably because the person has become aware of it.

What does this indicate? Well, it tells us that it takes consistent promotional messages before one could recognize your brand or your offering. Your business will need to be visible more often. And that should be your long-term goal. That should be your focus. You could be looking at a longer-term. The time horizon could even be longer than what you could expect, depending on how your business performs. And as an entrepreneur, you should consider such possibilities.

As a new entrepreneur, do you think you are now ready and set to explore the process? Would you like to take your brand (your product or offering) to the next level?

Now, the good thing is, you do not necessarily have to produce a TV commercial or radio commercial.

You will find that there is a different way of promoting your brand.

And you will be excited about it.

You will apply a marketing approach that would not be as expensive as how large-sized businesses would do their traditional marketing.

You probably have seen several viral videos on YouTube. Or you probably have been doing some social networking activities. How confident were you in using these social media tools? You could use any of these marketing tools to announce your company, your product, or your offering.

Many people haven't realized the full potential of online marketing and the power of social media.

Some of the reasons they say could be attributed to the fact that they lack time or knowledge.

What do you think you could do? What approaches would you use to make your customers aware of your brand or your company? What will you do to encourage customers to try out your product?

In essence, applying the right approach with micro enterprise marketing will take you to the process of satisfactorily serving one customer at a time.

* * *

Entrepreneurial Marketing Essentials

TARGET MARKET AS A DRIVING FORCE TO YOUR MICRO ENTERPRISE

With entrepreneurial marketing, an entrepreneur must look at the target market as a driving force to keep the micro enterprise going. Your marketing decisions must focus on your customers.

When you position your product or service, determine whether the strategy you are employing is viable. Would your customer be willing, would they have the capacity, and would they have the ability to buy?

You will need to adjust your marketing activities,

strategies and goals, depending on how your market reacts to your current offering.

You should look at some indicators that tell you how well the market is responding. Otherwise, you will have to think of other ways. You can ask, "What solutions would fit into the needs of my target market?".

COMMUNICATING SOLUTIONS AND VALUE TO YOUR CUSTOMERS

As an entrepreneur, you will have to think of several ways to promote your products to your customers. You can ask, "What would be the right message?". You will need to think of the right tone of your message. You will need to think of the right tools to deliver your message.

Always remember that a customer connects their emotion with their purchasing decisions. This emotional aspect should guide you when writing and presenting your message about your offerings to your customers.

Moreover, as an entrepreneur in this day and age, you must recognize that personal selling still plays a huge part in communicating your key message to your target customers.

You will need to connect directly to your customers. Your challenge is to think through the right approaches. That's the essence of being entrepreneurial. You could try different approaches. You could be dynamic yet could stay professional. You could think and reflect upon your customers' responses.

CREATING BETTER CUSTOMER EXPERIENCE

Customer service has never been more challenging than today. Customers actively use digital devices and spend more hours online.

Web users have been participating more and more in many online forums, and social media networks, and even online review sites. Customers can make or break any business today. Word of mouth can go viral, in such a way that can ruin people's reputation. On a bright note, it can increase followers and engagement.

What that means is - entrepreneurs and marketers must pay attention to their customers' engagement and online activities, as these aspects are crucial to their digital success.

How do you respond to customers when they approach you? Both offline and online?

You should be able to demonstrate your abilities to understand and relate to your customers' situation. You should show that you respect their responses, acknowledge any limitation and boundary they have set, and even recognize their frustration. You have to connect with them with empathy. You don't want to argue and even cause more conflict. You don't want to annoy your customers.

You will need to be more open and flexible with how you connect with them. You will need to carry on a two-way conversation. You will need to use more of and enhance your listening ability.

You could reflect upon each of the situations. And then ask this question: "How could I provide better customer service?".

The answer could be simple. "Be in the position of the customer.".

CREATING YOUR EFFECTIVE PRESENCE AND BRAND

With the right approach, entrepreneurial marketing can help your business create a strong presence or impression about you, your company, and your brand.

Remember, you have the unique ability to create solutions. Do not solely focus on products. But find a way to create the presentation with emphasis on the value one can get from using your product or your service.

When you create your presence (or brand) with your customers at the core of your approach, you will be able to connect with them a lot easier. They would, eventually, recognize that your business is the go-to place for them to find the right solutions to their problems or needs.

Review and evaluate your marketing mix and measure how they play out, considering your current marketing activities.

Create your marketing plan on a reasonable budget, employing practical use of marketing materials, digital marketing, and social media.

Chapter Five

Digital Marketing for Micro Enterprise

Digital Marketing for Micro Enterprise

CHAPTER 5

Embracing Digital Marketing

Competition and Global Presence

Key Components of Digital Marketing

Defining Digital Marketing

SEO and Its Impact to Your Content Marketing

How Your Customers Search Online

How Businesses Respond to Digital Marketing

Embracing Digital Marketing

Almost everyone is going digital these days. Well, at least when we see people around, we know that they use a combination of various electronic devices, such as computers, smartphones, and tablets. With that, it is worth noticing that many companies (be they small-sized, medium-sized, or large-sized) seemed to have been talking about the concept of digital marketing.

The question that would often come to our mind is, "How do I reach out to my target audience using these digital devices?".

The truth is – it is not easy as it may seem.

We live in a world in which we tend to get confused with so many available choices. We have to think and decide which one would best match our customers' needs. Given the rise of internet technologies, we are facing more challenges each day.

Consumers seem to have access to tons of information. As such, we could witness a tremendous impact on how to conduct our business in this digital era.

The question we should often ask, "How should I go about my marketing?".

Traditional marketing may not work anymore at some point. It will need to work alongside a combination of many other digital marketing tools.

Competition and Global Presence

Competition grew stronger. That is one thing we can, perhaps, think about these days.

Doing business has become even more challenging. The availability of digital technologies in almost every part of the world makes us wonder even more. "What would I do now?". "I would need to learn more about marketing.". "It would seem that digital marketing has a global scope.". Hence, the rise of global marketing in the digital age.

Many digital tools allow consumers to interact with businesses these days. Using social media, websites, and email can make the interaction going.

Publishing a website can make accessibility possible for the world to see. Creating your web presence does not just stay local. Many people from other regions or other countries can view your profile - whenever they want and wherever they are. They simply need to know your web address or even just your social media profile.

You can also create a more visible global web presence with the power of web content marketing.

However, digital marketing is not just about as easy as getting a website – or building content. There's a whole lot more to it.

Key Components of Digital Marketing

Let us explore digital marketing and its mechanisms.

We have witnessed the growth of web marketing and internet marketing in the past several years. These concepts happen to be the key to digital marketing. Many digital marketers are aware that web marketing and internet marketing can help shape the life of one's business in this digital era that we are in now.

Web Marketing (or website marketing) is the process of promoting a website using a variety of strategies to attract web users and to encourage them to stay on the website. Such strategies should allow users to learn about the company, the products, and other content.

On the other hand, **Internet Marketing** is the process of promoting products or services online using a combination of many digital tools. There are many tools that make up the concept of digital marketing. And that may come in various forms, including digital advertising, digital media, traditional media (television and radio), digital billboards, and games. Digital marketing can also use other digital channels, such as various social media platforms, mobile web applications, and email marketing.

> *Digital marketing is, therefore, a marketing concept that aims at communicating your brand (product or service) through the use of a combination of digital channels to reach your target market.*

Defining Digital Marketing

Digital marketing is, therefore, a marketing concept that aims at communicating your brand (product or service) through the use of a combination of digital channels to reach your target market.

Now let us do a little pondering here – **"Is your business digitally prepared to do marketing?"**

SEO and Its Impact to Your Online Content Marketing

Search Engine Optimization (or better known as 'SEO') is a creative process applied to a website with the objective of achieving visibility in the eyes of the search engines. Google has played a role in revolutionizing the idea of getting found online. And that would include the goal of being friendly with search engines.

When someone searches online and uses a set of keywords, relevant web pages (that have been indexed by search engines) may show up on the search results. The rank of web pages would depend on the degree of relevance of their content to the search.

The wonderful thing about search engine optimization is that when applied correctly and consistently, the web pages could be deemed an authority on their respective categories or industries.

SEO is attractive to a growing number of digital marketers, given its characteristics of being organic, natural, and cost-effective.

Now, what has got online content marketing to do with SEO?

Well, there's a relationship that goes between the two concepts.

When your web pages have relevant topics (that online users are searching for), and you have search-friendly content, and SEO elements have been appropriately applied, search engines will visit your site. Search engines will keep coming back to index your web pages each time you publish fresh content.

How Your Customers Search Online

Have you ever wondered about how your prospects or customers lookup for businesses, products, or services online?

It is not uncommon that consumers and internet users today use keywords to find what they are looking for when searching online.

Do you recognize what sort of keywords your company or organization could use so that your brand (or your company name) will show up in the search results? And when we say search results, we mean being on the first few pages, if not top position or ranking.

You must know that some internet users would only browse through the first few pages of the search results. And what is even apparent is that web pages that appear on the well-ranked positions have greater chances to be visited.

There is a tremendous opportunity in digital marketing. You just have to think through your marketing strategies.

Are you already incorporating online marketing?

Are you utilizing search engine optimization (SEO)?

What digital tools do you use?

How do you intend to explore the benefits that come with content marketing?

* * *

How Businesses Respond to Digital Marketing

In 2018, a US-based firm, Clutch, conducted a research study on digital marketing. In that research, some five-hundred-one (501) digital marketers of various businesses in the USA participated. And they responded to how they utilize digital marketing. (Herhold, 2018).[1]

Most of the businesses or eighty-three percent (83%) surveyed said that they find their efforts in digital marketing effective in achieving their business goal.

Most of the businesses or eighty-three percent (83%) said that they find their efforts in digital marketing effective in achieving their business goal.

[1]*Herhold, K. (2018, July 18). How Businesses Use Digital Marketing in 2018. Clutch. https://clutch.co/agencies/digital-marketing/resources/how-businesses-use-digital-marketing-2018*

In that study, there are three channels in digital marketing that emerged clearly as their top choices.

And that included **social media marketing** with eighty-one percent (81%), then **website** comes next – with seventy-eight percent (78%), and **email marketing** – at sixty-nine percent (69%).

The top three digital marketing channels: Social Media, Website, Email Marketing

There are apparent reasons why these top three digital marketing channels are the most preferred channels of marketers of businesses.

Many businesses would find that connecting to their targeted customers seemed a lot easier when using social media, website, and email marketing.

Consumers today are into online engagement. And using such channels would allow you to tell your story. You can demonstrate what your company is doing. And that your company is finding solutions to their needs.

You can discover more, such as how your customers use your products. And what it is that would appeal to their emotions.

And ultimately, you can deliver better. And you know how your company (or your brand) could effectively respond to the ever-growing market demands.

How else did businesses respond to the use of other digital marketing channels?

In that survey, we could see that display/banner ads followed with fifty-five percent (55%), then mobile apps with fifty-three percent (53%), and content marketing with fifty-three percent (53%).

So, how did the digital marketers respond to the use of Search Engine Optimization (SEO)?

Well, we were surprised by the result in SEO findings. The survey showed that only forty-four percent (44%) favoured SEO.

It goes to show that many businesses are still unaware of how SEO works. Some do not seem to realize that SEO must work alongside many digital channels. And that would include the use of website and content marketing tools. And as a whole, SEO could deliver better results.

* * *

How about your own experience with digital marketing? Are you familiar with the concept of SEO?

What are your thoughts about these digital marketing findings? Which of the digital marketing tools do you think would work best for your micro enterprise, considering cost-effectiveness?

Chapter Six

Low-Budget Marketing

Low-Budget Marketing

CHAPTER 6

PR: Press Release

Local Marketing

Mobile Marketing & Social Media

Creating a Website

Video Marketing

Email Marketing

Your Approach to Low-Budget Marketing

As an entrepreneur or owner of a micro enterprise, you will always be looking for ways in which you could save money, and yet you can still apply effective methods of promoting your enterprise.

Some cost-effective marketing tools that you can use - and that can help you achieve your marketing goals - are in the form of PR and press releases, local marketing, mobile marketing, social media, website marketing, video marketing, and email marketing.

You can utilize the digital tools, depending on your skills. You could use some tools on a do-it-yourself (DIY) approach. Or you could explore other platforms with the help of a specialist. The objective is to utilize the features and benefits of the tools to their fullest potential.

PR: Press Release

Is Writing and Distributing a Press Release Still Relevant in the Age of Digital Media?

We all have seen several businesses that thrive online.

Some of these successful companies have had some press coverage, at one point or another.

How does a company get such media coverage? How easy is it?

And why does a company need it anyway?

Press releases can create awareness of your company's activities, including the launch of new products, promotion, and brand campaigns.

Successful marketers and business owners know the importance of using press releases.

Seven Reasons for Writing and Distributing Press Releases

Here are seven reasons for using, writing, and distributing press releases:

1. **To support your company's communication strategy.** It forms part of your content marketing strategy.
2. **To support your branding goals.** By using press releases, your target market can become aware of your brand messages.
3. **To help in building your industry authority and leadership.** You can become the source of information relevant to the industry in which you operate.
4. **To support your online search visibility and ranking.** With press release distribution, many

other influential people, bloggers, journalists, business owners, and marketers interested in the information can link to the news release and share the message through their preferred media platforms.

5. **To educate your customers.** Many people trust news more than the paid form of communication, which is advertising. If you intend to educate your customers, a newsworthy release of information can be a better way to approach it.

6. **To create a public announcement.** The press release content can become a public record and can serve as a reference. Whenever a web user searches online on your targeted keywords, there's a good possibility that your news content can appear up on the search results.

7. **To support your overall digital strategy.** A news release distributed through a news service can help support your overall digital presence.

Professional PR Writing

How can someone write news and press releases like a PRO?

Having some professional skills is essential when creating a good story, such as news, publicity announcements, and press releases.

Acquired professional writing skills can help make a huge difference. Getting the professional message out is integral for any business organization.

Ever wonder how skilled journalists write a newsworthy story, publicity announcements, and press releases?

Professionals know the vital aspects in PR writing that can create a well-crafted story, and that can also get attention and attract conversation and shares through other media platforms. You might want to consult with a PR consultant or writer to accomplish your PR goal.

A professional press release writer understands vital elements in writing, such as the inverted pyramid, answers to readers' questions or the 5 Ws and H, and writing a good headline.

Press Release Distribution

If you are ready to send your press release out to the news media outlets, you can now decide to use the service of a PR distribution company.

* * *

Local Marketing

You probably have encountered the acronym SEO a gazillion times.

Many people, at this point, must have heard of SEO and how important it is in one's business, given that we are in the digital age.

However, is everyone aware of how to properly utilize SEO?

All right SEO (or if we must emphasize search engine optimization) is the process of optimizing your website (or web pages) both on-page and off-page.

The purpose of SEO boils down to getting your website found online through search engines.

Google holds the description of being the biggest search engine. And as such, website owners strive to make their websites as relevant and search-friendly as possible. Therefore, they must adhere to Google's set of rules and practices in applying search engine optimization.

There are a few more search engines web users would also use. That would include Bing and Yahoo, and a few other small search engines.

And now comes the Local SEO. And why would one need to focus on getting found locally?

Just because your web presence may reach the global sphere because of the use of the internet, it does not necessarily mean that the whole world - the world wide web or anyone who can access your site is your market.

If your customers are local, and so is your approach. You have to be visible where they are.

Using Local SEO is a practical approach to market your business 24/7 online.

Such an approach can help boost your presence to your local customers at their convenient time, using their computers or electronic devices, such as tablets and mobile phones.

Do you need to target a set of population, community, or neighbourhood in your geographic location?

You may need to concentrate on Local SEO as one of your digital marketing approaches to promote your product or service.

Local SEO Tools Can Help You Improve Your Online Presence and Keep You on Track

It is worth noticing how many businesses in the United States and Canada, as well as other countries in Europe and Asia, have been using local SEO tools.

And that would include those tools developed by Google (also known as Google My Business).

Some other Local SEO tools developed by various software companies have also been made available. Some of these tools may be worth giving a try.

Such Local SEO tools can help businesses and marketers manage, monitor, and review their local SEO performance.

You could find an all-in-one Local SEO reporting platform that provides access to a variety of SEO tools. Business owners or digital marketers can view their local SEO data in a specified location dashboard.

When you use a Local SEO platform, you would be able to test out those tools that would help track your website's performance, including its organic ranking, local ranking, and even mobile ranking. You would also be able to check on which sites link to your website. You would as well be able to do a website audit based on your target keywords. And then, you would be able to assess the overall results.

It also allows users to audit citations and information (such as the name of the company, address, and phone number details – also referred to as NAP). You would be able to build or add local citations. It will also allow you to generate SEO audits and reports.

Some platforms can also help work alongside other digital tools, such as Google My Business performance monitoring tool, the integration of Google Analytics, and social media monitoring tools.

Getting listed on local online directories can get your business and website found online. Your customers can connect with you using the contact information on the online listing.

Another digital tool you might want to look into is monitoring customers' reviews. Knowing what your customers say about you would help you respond strategically. It will also guide you about your customers' behaviour and what else you could do to improve your performance.

In other words, this kind of digital tool can help you monitor your Online Reputation, given that you can be on top of customer reviews. You can opt into receiving alerts each time your customers leave a comment, or review about you, your service, and your business.

Such tools could guide you on what you can do to deal with issues or concerns. And how your business can ultimately improve - to achieve customer satisfaction.

Finally, you would be able to connect and engage with your avid customers and fans if and when an opportunity calls for it. After all, it's always better to be proactive and prepared.

Some solutions providers would allow a new user to start using the tool with a free or trial account. You would be able to test out and explore the tools. In this way, you would know and assess how the tools can help with your business.

* * *

Mobile Marketing & Social Media:

How the World of Mobile Marketing Can Impact Your Micro Enterprise

As a micro entrepreneur or small business owner, you might wonder about how the world of mobile marketing can help your micro enterprise become more engaging with your customers.

People Love Connecting

You realize that most consumers these days are mobile phone users. It's like almost every person you meet around has been communicating through their mobile device.

People who own a smartphone or tablet would find it convenient to find information through the mobile web.

Similar to using the desktop computer, mobile users can also expect to have a good if not better user experience navigating through the mobile web.

Social Media Network

People get personal access to almost every important aspect in their daily experiences using mobile devices, such as tablets and smartphones.

That is why mobile users love social media.

People love to connect to their loved ones in an instant. So, if your customers use mobile devices to access their social media, why wouldn't you?

Go - where your customers are.

Finding Local Businesses

And how about finding or locating businesses, retail shops, dental and medical clinics, grocers, restaurants, and food stores?

Yes, people would like to have easy access to their nearby shops. And how do they do that using their smartphones?

Mobile web users can look up information and other applications through the mobile web using search engines, such as Google. Mobile users would use keywords and specific locations (just like when they are using desktop computers) to search and browse the web.

Competing for Targeted Keywords

Many websites would compete for similar or familiar keywords (that you may also use) to show up on the first page if not the number one position in the search results.

Businesses with websites that are mobile-friendly and search engine-friendly, providing better navigational experience, would gain the most attention from the targeted mobile web users.

Businesses would then need to review and reflect upon their mobile web presence. "What should I do to provide a much better mobile web experience? How do I optimize my website?".

* * *

Creating a Website

How to Easily Create a Website for Your Micro Enterprise

> *Website ranked second on digital marketing to invest on, with seventy-eight percent (78%) most favoured by digital marketers of businesses.*

Website is one of the primary channels of choice on digital marketing for most small businesses.

And as mentioned earlier regarding the 2018 survey (conducted by Clutch), Website ranked second on digital marketing to invest on - with seventy-eight percent (78%) most favoured by digital marketers of businesses, next to social media that earned eighty-one percent (81%).

We were not surprised by such findings. Website is a very vital component of digital marketing, no matter how big or small your business. It is imperative for customers (or clients) to access information online. Customers could learn about your business, your products, and your contact details in an instant. Website is one of the tools, if not the primary one, that could help you fulfill such objectives.

In this digital age, many consumers would do their research online on various products before deciding which products or brands they would purchase. Those businesses with well-presented, well-optimized websites could easily attract attention based on the kind of content they publish. Many consumers are looking for useful content that would help answer their questions.

> *"Creating a website is one of the essential digital marketing tasks a small business must look into if they seek to inform, communicate and connect with their target customers."*

Creating a website is one of the essential digital marketing tasks a small business must look into if they seek to inform, communicate and connect with their target customers.

The good thing about creating a website these days is that it has become easier than ever to find an easy-to-use web platform to house your content.

What website publishing platform do you use?

Many web publishing platforms are available in the market today.

By web browsing or searching online with keywords such as web design platform or website builder, you would instantly see various web pages appearing on searches that talk about website building.

That is how easy it would seem to create a website in this day and age.

It was not like the same several years ago when designing a website seems that way complicated - that you would need to start from scratch with the necessary web programming, technical, and creative skills. You would need a web programmer in addition to hiring a web designer.

However, not all web publishing platforms are created equal. In using WordPress, for example, you might need a WordPress specialist, or web developer, especially if you are not familiar with the web design platform.

Have you ever used the CMS platform WordPress for your web content publishing?

How easy is it for you to work on WordPress?

Have you found a powerful hosting that could manage your WordPress?

If not, what web publishing platform do you think would you use?

If you are looking to create a new website, you have several options to approach that task. Are you searching for a web design platform or like an alternative to WordPress, but you have no idea about HTML coding or any type of web programming?

You can try some intuitive web platforms, even if you are new to this web design thing. You can open an account on a trial basis. You can navigate the platform, explore its features and see if the platform meets your website needs.

Some website builders could offer free trials for seven (7) days, fourteen (14) days, and thirty (30) days.

You could familiarize yourself with the platform to check if it serves your purpose. Some web platforms could offer free hosting. But they do not allow the use of your domain name.

You could start with a minimal hosting package, and you could be good to go - and you can even use your branding.

In that way, it will help you establish your web presence with a more professional look.

Website owners would be able to tap into their creativity in designing a website. Therefore, depending on their skills and level of comfort, website owners can choose a do-it-yourself (DIY) option.

Have you used a web design platform with a do-it-yourself (DIY) option? Or have you worked with a web designer to create your website? Reflect upon your experience.

Ultimately, this would be your call.

You will have to look into the pros and cons of the direction you are taking for creating your website.

But if your budget would allow it, it is worth a try if you could work with a designer that can help you accomplish this web design thing.

With working with a web designer, you do not have to worry about the technicality and design of your website. You would be able to do other essential aspects of your business. You would be able to concentrate on growing your business - attending to your day-to-day operation.

Your objective should be to create a website in which your customers can navigate with ease. The website should allow them to have a better user experience.

* * *

Video Marketing

Video marketing is a practical yet creative method of promoting your presence in the digital space.

Depending on your business, you can create various types of videos. Such videos could include product videos, company profile videos, and promotional videos.

Why create promo videos?

Well, videos are very in demand today, more than ever. Great video presentations can attract consumers like crazy.

An entrepreneur in this day and age should be doing video marketing.

Is your business online? Would your business be doing some promotion? If so, then video marketing could be part of your digital marketing mix.

With video marketing, your business will stand out and outshine your competitors. Your target customers can quickly get to know you, your company, and your products or services.

The more visible you are - the more customers will become aware of your brand.

Did you know that, more and more, customers these days are likely going to buy a product (or subscribe to a service) after watching some video presentations?

Simply put, video marketing using promo videos can help you get engaged with your target audience quickly and get your message effectively.

You can use a video creation platform online - that comes with hundreds, if not thousands, of video templates.

Subscribing to a video creation platform is becoming more affordable these days.

The video platform allows video creators to make videos in a few easy steps. You can create sales promotional videos and highlight your brand.

Some video maker platforms allow video creators to create social videos that are great for Facebook, Instagram, and YouTube.

A video creator can create horizontal videos (16 x 9), vertical videos (9 x 16) and square videos (1 x 1).

A video maker platform can give you access to several video templates. Such templates are ideal for business/corporate, education, entertainment, music, fashion, beauty, sports, fitness, wellness, food and restaurant services, real estate, events, holidays, and occasions, and more.

With many choices available these days, many entrepreneurs and online marketers could explore how to create stunning videos to impress their target audience.

So whether you are an experienced video marketer or beginning to explore how to integrate video marketing into your overall digital marketing strategy, you could discover many possibilities.

COMMUNICATE YOUR MESSAGE VIA VIDEOS

Doing video presentations, no doubt, has become one of the most practical ways, if not the most entertaining way, to communicate your message to your audience.

You can actively navigate several options to connect via videos. Communicating via a video conference and even conducting webinars seem to attract many audiences online.

VIDEO PRODUCTION AND EDITING SKILLS

How easy is it to make a video these days?

Wouldn't video marketing require some kind of expertise and creativity?

Having the skills and knowledge about video production and editing could be an asset. Nevertheless, you could always explore the process of how to create videos. Why not check out some online courses on video production, photography, and video editing?

However, you do not need to worry to that extent. Creating videos can take so much of your time.

Some people can find creating videos just fine, while others struggle with exploring concepts and creativity.

Unless this is the type of thing you specialize in, sometimes, it would be better off to leave it to a specialist who can help you with your video marketing campaigns.

You could, perhaps, hire someone who could offer reasonable fees. You could also do an exchange of your service or product for a video project with a video marketing specialist who then might need your service or product. It can be a win-win deal.

HOW TO VIDEOS

So now, are you thinking of creating a video that aims to explain to your audience how to accomplish tasks?

How about making a tutorial or educational video that guides your audience to learn about your product (or anything that you could think about or share - for that matter)?

You can find some inspiration - in seeing some video samples that could help speed up your creative process. Some video creators are into the idea of exploring how-to videos using a simple online video editing platform.

Some beginners, and even experienced video creators, would prefer to explore some video templates. Such video templates could help them design and produce their video project.

There are several video projects a video creator could create with a video editor or video creation platform.

You can explore some video ideas for inspiration. You can create your version, depending on your type of business.

- Marketing Video Tutorial
- Real Estate Videos - How to Find the Right Agent
- Easy Makeup Tutorial
- Wellness at Work
- How to Choose the Best Smartphone
- Top Web Design Tips for Beginners
- How to Protect Your Home Daily
- Five Ways to Improve Your Management Skills
- Ten Tips for Nutritious Food Diet
- How to Develop Good Learning Habits
- How to Manage Your Resources Well in Your Business
- How to Start an E-Commerce Website
- How to Quickly Speak English as a Second Language
- How to Start a Self-help Podcast
- How to Take a Stunning Selfie Shot

    ...and more...

You could think of many other video project ideas to present what you do and what your audience needs to see.

What is Video Hosting?

It's no secret that videos have been making waves since the beginning of the digital era. Videos are created not only for personal consumption but for the use of businesses as well.

Video marketing is a marketing tool that could be part of the overall digital marketing strategy of a business.

Are you already using videos to communicate your message to your audience? If so, how do you present your videos to your targeted audience?

How do you showcase your videos on your website? What video hosting service do you use?

What is video hosting, anyway?

Defining Video Hosting

Video hosting is an online service that would allow users to upload and play back their video content.

As such, video hosting creates and enables an online video platform so that your audience can view your videos.

Is Your Website Capable of Hosting Videos?

There are website hosts that could allow website owners to upload their videos on their platform. Most often than not, however, the result may not be satisfying.

Even if you research around, you will find that those who attempt to do it that way may not have a good experience. That method is also known as self-hosting.

What is Video Self-hosting?

> *Video self-hosting refers to putting video content, or in this case a video file, to the same web hosting provider or web server that hosts your website.*

Video self-hosting refers to putting video content, or in this case a video file, to the same web hosting provider or web server that hosts your website. On the same server is where you would also upload your other digital content, like photos or images.

The truth about video self-hosting is that - not all web servers or web hosting providers are created alike.

Some web hosting providers or servers would not allow video uploads as part of their services.

Some would put limits or restrictions on the video file. Web hosts or providers would not provide video hosting on some websites hosted on a shared server.

And you may wonder, "Why would video hosting not work well on a shared web environment?".

Some of the reasons include limitations on server bandwidth, storage space, file size restrictions, video slow loading, and a lot more.

Is there any website service provider out there that can help with at least a simple video hosting?

How should we present videos using a website?

It is always a lot easier to host a video through a third-party video hosting provider such as YouTube and Vimeo. You could simply embed videos onto your website.

As an alternative, however, you could also check on various website builders that include a video element feature.

If you are already using a website builder, you might want to check if there's a video element included in your subscription. Some would even have the feature that can host HD videos.

If you are beginning to explore a site editor of your site builder, you can try using the video element for your video uploads.

Depending on your website hosting plan, a video element may be available with select subscriptions.

Video Hosting with YouTube or Vimeo

Hosting your videos through YouTube or Vimeo is your best option, especially if video hosting is currently not available with your web hosting.

But even if your website is capable of hosting your videos, you may still want to consider using YouTube or Vimeo. It's way simple and easy to embed your videos on your website or blog.

The important thing is you're able to showcase your video presentations through your website.

* * *

Email Marketing

Email marketing is a cost-effective marketing approach for a micro enterprise. Many people use email for communication. Therefore, most would visit their inbox regularly.

If done right, creating email marketing campaigns can deliver results.

When doing email marketing, with automation software, you could send messages, you could access reports, and then you could measure performance. Using automation software, you could analyze your customers (or clients) better and think of how you could improve on your strategies for customer engagement.

Many automation software providers of email marketing services have affordable packages or subscriptions. Some could even offer the use of the software for free, although with limited features. But this can already help you get started and explore the platform.

There are different ways in which email marketing can help in your overall marketing goals.

It could help build your brand, credibility, and trust. People would only want to receive communication from the people or company they find credible.

So if clients or customers opt into receiving email messages from you, that would be a good sign.

Email marketing can help strengthen your image and the relationship you have built with them.

You can connect and engage with your customers (or clients) with a personal touch.

You can reach your customers with the use of any device, such as mobile devices. You could also make your email marketing work alongside your mobile marketing and your social media campaigns.

Email marketing can help you save time when using automation software. You get organized better and improve your customer communication.

As you start and grow your customer base, you will be able to introduce your products (or your services) and communicate the features and benefits of your offerings. Doing email marketing helps improve your visibility with your customers. Consequently, it can help boost sales.

Email marketing also helps in increasing traffic to your website as clients or customers click on the links from your message.

Your message should therefore be exciting and should add value to what they already know.

Finally, always approach email marketing with your target customers or clients in mind. In doing so, you will benefit a lot when creating your message before hitting the send button.

* * *

Your Approach to Low-Budget Marketing

For many entrepreneurs, doing marketing does not come easily. They go from one approach to another without a clear picture of how it would turn out, whether it would bring in traffic to their website or bring in more leads, and even so, sales.

Achieving sales goals would depend on how you approach marketing.

Most of the available low-cost digital tools, such as the use of social media, web content, videos, email marketing, and search engine optimization, can result in bringing in traffic to your website, can create better customer engagement, and ultimately, can result in getting leads and sales.

Choosing the right marketing tools for your micro business requires that you understand how each of these tools will help you achieve your marketing objectives in the long run. You can use a combination of these tools and analyze results.

Would you use the tools with a do-it-yourself (DIY) approach? Or would you hire an expert or consultant in using the tools to make use of the features and benefits to the fullest? You may need to re-evaluate your overall marketing approaches and review your budget or adjust, depending on the outcome.

3

HOW TO GROW YOUR MICRO ENTERPRISE

Chapter Seven

How to Grow Your Micro Business

How to Grow Your Micro Business

CHAPTER 7

What Does Business Growth Mean To You?

Business Challenges and Growth Strategies

What Does Business Growth Mean To You?

So you think you are ready now to take your micro enterprise to the next level? That is when the word 'growth' would come into the picture.

What is business growth? How would you define it?

Growth could refer to many different things. Small business owners could look at growth based on many aspects of their enterprise.

Growth could mean something to one entrepreneur but could be different to another entrepreneur.

When you start to think about growth, you could look at many areas of your business.

You could think about growth in terms of revenue increase.

Let us say your micro business earned a gross income of thirty thousand dollars (30K) last year. This year, you could think of a twenty percent increase, based on that income from the previous year.

You could also look at your sales. You might want to consider increasing sales volume. You could add new clients (or customers).

You could also start to think of adding help or support, like having an employee, to assist you in your business operation.

Likewise, you could consider the idea of expansion in terms of your business location or by adding a new branch.

Also, another aspect that you might want to look into in terms of growth is innovation. You could add new products or product lines to your current offerings.

We could go on and on - adding to the list of possibilities.

The bottom line is, you have to realize that growth reflects the kind of goals you want to achieve.

Why do you seek growth?

Is it about the money thing?

Is it about enjoying freedom?

Is it about being able to make your decisions?

Is it about exploring your creative expression?

Is it about being able to work on your passions without needing validation and approval from others?

Is it about recognition of being or becoming a successful entrepreneur in your chosen industry?

You could perhaps think of other possible reasons. And whatever reason you might have for seeking growth, that would serve as your driving force to keep going. Ultimately, you could achieve your intended level of business growth.

Given your situation, what are you thinking of in terms of growth for your micro business?

* * *

Business Challenges and Growth Strategies

As you think about your plan for business growth, it would be imperative that you are aware of your situation. You will need to be able to assess where your business stands in its life cycle.

Business Life Cycle

Beginning Stage >
Growth > Maturity > Decline

At this point, you must have passed the beginning stage, as you now seek growth.

Growth Stage

Just because you have achieved some level of growth does not necessarily mean everything would be rosy. Of course, growth comes with some kind of challenges, depending on your business.

You must be aware of some possible challenges that may come your way. How would you be able to handle it if ever, such challenging circumstances would occur?

As an entrepreneur, you could encounter unexpected scenarios in the business environment. You could be into some challenges that would need urgent responses.

You could encounter some cases that would require fulfillment in product demand, and even modification in pricing and changes in sales channels and distribution chains.

How about financing? That can also be a challenge. Would you have enough source of funds to sustain and respond to demand?

How are you going to manage resources? Would you now delegate some tasks in your operation and hire staff to keep up with the business demand? Would you consider sub-contractors to help you deliver the products and other requirements?

What kind of systems would you put in place so that it would be easier to track your activities, including the money aspect, day-to-day operations, and other tasks necessary to respond to your business growth?

Maturity

Some businesses reach this maturity stage in which the challenge is - how to find other areas of growth. You would need to avoid any tendency to be complacent.

You will need to keep pushing beyond your current situation.

You will need to seek out new ways to discover new horizons.

You would need to be more creative than ever.

You would need to think of strategies that are vital to your business' longevity.

Decline

Some businesses in their respective industry could reach some point of decline.

We could cite an example in the area of media and publishing. If we look at the print business, for example, a magazine business, or newspaper business, we could see that many companies have now been seeking out new ways to keep their business rolling and be in demand.

Businesses that could not keep up with the demands in the digital environment could go into **slow decline**.

They must therefore think of new approaches in many areas of their business. They may need to evolve into a new form that could be more attractive to their target audience.

As a business owner, your challenge would be - how would you respond and still be relevant? What changes will you undertake so that you can keep your business going - despite the economic circumstances?

In the recent COVID-19 pandemic that has shaken the world and has brought global health crisis, many businesses have been affected. Some establishments had to downsize. Some had decided to limit their operations.

Some of these circumstances could lead many businesses to face rapid decline.

Some businesses could explore the idea of **reinventing and seeing possibilities in other areas** of the industry.

The challenge a business faces at such a point would be about pursuing new growth that could lead later to either rapid growth or maturity, depending on how fast or slow a business moves.

Chapter Eight

Your Strategic Plan and Your Business Growth

Your Strategic Plan and Your Business Growth

CHAPTER 8

Why Is There a Need for Strategic Planning?

How to Create Your Strategic Plan

Key Business Growth Essentials

A Closer Look at Marketing for Business Growth

Conclusion

Why Is There a Need for Strategic Planning?

Sometimes, you can't help but wonder, as a micro business owner, why do you have to go through some kind of formality when you think about planning and operating your business. After all, we know that with a small business, such as a micro enterprise, it could be just a simple operation. As an entrepreneur, you are aware that you may have limited resources.

So, why is there a need for strategic planning in micro enterprise? What is strategic planning, anyway?

> *Strategic planning in micro enterprise is an entrepreneurial process whereby entrepreneurs outline their strategies and goals for their business.*

Strategic planning in micro enterprise is an entrepreneurial process whereby entrepreneurs outline their strategies and goals for their business. When doing strategic planning, an entrepreneur would know the direction and the plan of actions to undertake.

What comes with strategic planning is the decision-making process. It would also identify and describe all the resources needed to execute your strategy. The strategic plan would, in essence, describe the manner in how you would take charge and take control of the operation. The plan would also identify other aspects of your business, such as the internal and external factors that may influence the direction and operation of your business.

How to Create Your Strategic Plan

Strategic planning need not be complicated. After all, it should remind and guide you what you want for your business.

What is your vision for your micro business? What are your strengths? What are your limitations? What could some opportunities and challenges be in the industry? What are your goals for your micro business?

You do not have to be overwhelmed with the process. Remember, it should serve your purpose and not the other way around.

You should look at it as an outline or script, just like how a filmmaker would do a film project. A script would be essential to guide the entire filmmaking process. You would need to find the answers to "Who would do what, where, how, when?".

Then review and assess the process.

You will need to make adjustments, depending on how you are performing so far.

What are the limitations and challenges that could come along the way?

How do you go to the point where you should be - after resolving one challenge after another?

Reflect upon the whole process, again, especially when you find complexity or new challenges in your current situation. How do you simplify? What risks or threats do you see? How about opportunities? Understand where you are now. Where do you want to go? How?

Let us explore a guide on how to create your strategic plan for your micro business:

VISION > SWOT > GOALS

Creating Your Vision Statement

When writing your vision statement, you would express the purpose of your micro business. You would need to identify what it exactly does and what values shape and guide your enterprise.

You should review and update (if and when it is necessary) your vision statement from time to time as changes take place in your business.

What is SWOT Analysis?

When working on your SWOT analysis, you would need to look at all the significant factors surrounding your micro business. The SWOT acronym would stand for your business' Strengths, Weaknesses, Opportunities, and Threats.

When you look at all these four aspects of your business, you are also looking at the overall industry whereby you operate your business. An example is - if you have a catering business, you will have to look at the food industry in general. Then, you will need to focus closely on a subset of that industry (which is the catering business). Or if you are in the real estate brokerage business, you will have to be knowledgeable, not only in the geographic area you specialize but the overall real estate market as well.

You will have to look at industry regulations, changes in the economy and market demand.

Then, look at the challenges or possible threats.

What opportunities could you find there?

What are the limitations or weaknesses of your business?

How can your micro business fit in? What are its strengths (or advantages over other existing micro businesses)?

Evaluating your SWOT would help you come up with your strategies for your micro business.

Setting Goals for Your Micro Business

In setting your goals, you will need to refer back to the vision statement and the SWOT analysis you created earlier.

Now, in creating and writing your micro business goals, you would need to check on some criteria. These criteria would help you when thinking of your objectives and writing down your goals.

Are the goals specific?

Are the goals measurable?

Are the goals attainable?

Are the goals relevant?

Are the goals timely?

Are you ready to create your strategic plan and qualify your goals, considering the given criteria?

You can refer to the (following) guide that we use as an example.

STRATEGIC PLAN FOR MY MICRO BUSINESS

(Name of your Micro Business)

BUSINESS VISION STATEMENT

What's your business purpose?

Why are you doing this business?

Whom do you want to serve?

What products or services do you offer?

What is your business philosophy? Or what values would matter to you?

SWOT ANALYSIS

On Strengths and Opportunities:

Analyze what will help with your business - both the internal and external environment.

On Weaknesses and Threats:

Analyze what will hurt, damage, or danger your business, both the internal and external environment.

BUSINESS GOALS

Looking at your Vision Statement and SWOT Analysis, you can now set your goals.

What do you want to accomplish, say in three years? How about five years?

Remember, you need to qualify your goals. And make sure that these goals are specific, measurable, attainable, relevant, and timely.

Simply put, when creating your goals, remember the SMART acronym, and you are good to go.

* * *

Key Business Growth Essentials

Your micro business growth essentials would include at least four major areas, Resources Management, Finances, Operations Management and Marketing.

Resources Management

Resources management is vital in looking at your overall business growth. As a business owner, you would need to be open-minded and flexible and adjust your management approach.

You would need to apply different approaches that would make sense to you and for your business. You would need to manage your resources, such as your time, people, office, and financial resources.

Finances

As the chief person in your business, it is your responsibility to ensure that you have sound financial management.

You should be able to determine and understand the systems in place in your business.

Also, you should look into your company's financial statements. You should be on top of your business cash-flow forecasts. You should read and review your financial data as often as may be necessary.

How well do you oversee accounting and bookkeeping? How do you go about your taxation?

Depending on your needs, you might also want to consult with an accounting professional or tax advisor to address your specific situation.

Operations Management

Managing your company's operation is crucial in achieving your business goals.

How do you take control so that all business aspects function smoothly?

Do you have some guidelines that you have set for your day-to-day operations? At some point, or as your business grows and starts to add some help or employees, these guidelines will need to be accessible, even with just a simple handbook or manual.

Having a written procedure or guidelines for your business would work to your advantage in the long run.

You would be able to guide and manage your business organization well and no matter its size, whether you have one or two or five employees.

Marketing & Sales

As a business owner or entrepreneur, you recognize that marketing is one of the most vital aspects when starting, managing, and growing an enterprise.

For small businesses, like a micro enterprise, marketing could refer to attracting, getting, and keeping customers so that sales could keep coming in.

The general objective, therefore, of a micro enterprise in terms of marketing and sales would be to ensure that customers (or clients) are happy and satisfied with the products and services. You would be able to close deals and keep sales flowing, even if you just start with one sale, especially if the customer has had a good experience with your products or services.

The question that you could perhaps reflect upon would be: "How would I be able to generate enough interest in the mind of every customer?".

Customers could be your ally. They could spread the word about your product. They could talk about the benefits that go along with the product or service.

You could get - one customer after another. And the cycle could go on. You could be getting good referrals, which then could lead to more sales.

Customers could serve as your walking marketing tool. After all, they could share with others their experience in using your product or service. They could go to social media networks and other social forums. Their testimonials could influence other people in your target niche.

Customers' active participation in the digital space, such as social media, web forums, and online review sites, could influence other consumers and web users. Such social engagement could either boost or ruin a business reputation.

So, it is better off to put your target market at the core of your marketing mix.

When you work on your marketing for your business, you go through a process. The marketing process entails several tasks.

When you work on your marketing for your business, you go through a process. The marketing process entails several tasks.

These tasks would be to analyze the needs of your customers, to communicate your solutions (by way of products or services), and to deliver such solutions at the right time and place.

Customer experience is of paramount importance, more than ever, and therefore, marketers and entrepreneurs should give attention to how well they could respond to their customers' needs.

* * *

A Closer Look at Marketing for Business Growth

By now, you may start to appreciate the wonder of marketing. In essence, marketing is a component in growing your micro business. But, you may still think about some other things: "When, where, why, and how would I go about it?".

Okay, you have your products. You have your target customers. Now, you may wonder, "How many more tasks should I carry out to fulfill marketing for business growth?".

When you were at the early stages of your business activities, you must have been doing already some aspects of marketing. But as your small business moves in your intended direction, you would need to analyze and review (if possible) how well you have done so far.

Now, just because your early stages of marketing turned out okay and brought you some reasonable sales and revenue, it does not automatically mean it will continue the same way.

Many aspects of business growth can be associated with change.

In our earlier topic on Business Challenges and Growth Strategies, we recognize that a business could go through a life cycle.

A business could be in any of the three vital stages: Growth, Maturity, and Decline.

As an entrepreneur, where could you be at this point?

As you pursue business growth, you will need to look at your marketing goals. And what comes with that is - the need to identify the current situation in your micro business. Have your needs changed? Remember, what might have worked in the earlier stages of your micro business may not work in the present time.

Some marketing aspects that you might need to look into would be your target market, your product or service, your sales channel, your pricing, and even your marketing budget.

TARGET MARKET

As you pursue growth, you would need to assess the market you are trying to reach. Part of your marketing tasks would be to define (or redefine) your marketing goals.

You would need to know whether you are still working on targeting the same market. Or would you need to redefine that part?

For example, when you look at your target market, you could consider whether you would like to maintain your current customer demographics or you would like to target a new segment of customers.

Where are your customers based - local, regional or global?

PRODUCT OR SERVICE

On your current product offerings, are you adding a new product line? Do you have new and more affordable sources of these new products or raw materials (to produce your product)? Or are you doing the opposite - trying to get rid of products that are no longer viable in the market?

PRICE

When you look at your pricing strategy, are you thinking of providing your products with a higher price or lower price?

In other words, how dramatic are the changes in your product's pricing?

Do you cater now to a select few who could afford higher prices? Or the case is different as you now plan to reach out to consumers in a lower-income bracket.

Your marketing should reflect your current price point.

You will need to develop new marketing campaigns if and when there are changes to your prices.

SALES CHANNEL

Your sales channel is dependent on the specific market you are targeting.

For example, if you are used to offering your service or product for the business-to-consumer (B2C) market, and later you decided to target the business-to-business (B2B) segment, you will need to review and revise your marketing plan to reflect the actual target market.

MARKETING BUDGET

What is your current marketing budget?

Have you increased your budget since six months ago or last year?

Have you allocated more on digital marketing? In what area of marketing have you reduced your budget?

You would need to review your marketing spending. You would need to see if, indeed, you are allocating funds in that area of marketing that could deliver the best return.

* * *

Why Is There a Need for Market Research

Your business, depending on its current situation, might need market research to guide you when creating, if not, revising your marketing plan.

Market research would be essentially necessary if and when you experience dramatic changes in some aspects of your business.

When working on your marketing mix, you will need to put your target market at the core of all other parts in the mix.

Marketing components are dependent on how your target market responds to your offering, given your products and pricing. You would need to make some adjustments or modifications in your approaches, depending on how the business environment progresses.

Market research could give you some idea about your customers' behaviour. It could tell you whether your customers could accept or not what you provide in the market.

Market research could also help you understand your customers' varying needs. How small or large is that segment in the market? What is the current situation in that niche?

Is there an increasing demand from this market? Or is this market losing interest in what you provide, and therefore could decline at some point?

Where are the customers based - local or international? Who makes up the demographics?

How about the purchasing behaviour? What would be the customers' payment preference? How frequent would customers buy? How much could customers afford? Would customers buy monthly, quarterly, or annually?

How To Do Your Market Research

Conducting your market research may be done through primary market research or secondary market research.

With Primary Research, you directly conduct the study. It means you would gather the data yourself, or you would hire someone to do it.

Primary Research can be carried out, for example, by doing consumer surveys, conducting focus groups, and asking respondents through social media.

With Secondary Research, you would gather information through other sources. You could access research works of various entities, such as government agencies, national organizations, and industry associations. You could also find relevant works of other market research companies.

* * *

Learning and Analyzing Competition in Your Industry

After focusing on many aspects of marketing, it is about time that you further analyze how other companies in your industry do their marketing.

What marketing tools and methods do they use?

Do they focus more on advertising?

How about publishing press releases? What other PR activities do they do?

Are they active in social media?

Have you researched your direct competitors online? Did you see their websites?

What keywords do you think they use so that web users could find their sites online?

Given all that you have researched on your competitors, what do you think is their impact on the marketplace?

What could you learn from your competitors' performance? How would you make your business stand out from your competitors?

* * *

Assessing Your Marketing Strategy for Business Growth

Considering all the many concepts that we have explored, what strategies do you think would work for your micro business?

Just remember that with each strategy that you come up with, you will need to assess and ask the following:

Will this strategy work with my current situation, considering my available resources? And can these fulfill my marketing objectives?

- Manpower resources - Who would do the tasks? (In most cases, you will be the one; or you can assign someone else, possibly, a part-time employee or sub-contractor.)

- Budget - Would executing this 'strategy' be within my budget?

- Target market - Would this strategy satisfy the needs of my target clients or customers?

- And finally, will this strategy help me reach my goals for my micro business?

Conclusion

Entrepreneurship can be an exciting adventure if you know how to navigate the many roads to reaching your goals.

As an entrepreneur and prime mover of your micro enterprise, it is expected of you to have your entrepreneurial spirit. Remember, just because a person has started a micro business does not automatically translate to having the right characteristics of an entrepreneur.

A person can learn and acquire entrepreneurial skills. But, a person to be entrepreneurial, in essence, must have the ability to be creative in finding solutions.

Entrepreneurs believe that everything starts from their vision. They must have the confidence to make their vision happen.

They believe they have their unique capability to achieve their goals. They know that they can do it.

They are ready to pursue entrepreneurship with the right entrepreneurial mindset.

A micro enterprise owner must understand the concept of marketing and how its components must blend. They must go through the process of working on the right mix to come up with the solutions.

Entrepreneurs are always open to ideas. But to determine whether these ideas would work on your micro enterprise is another thing.

The bottom line, if you know your target market well, and you can provide your solutions (in the form of products or services), and you listen to feedback and encourage communication, you would be able to achieve your business goals down the road.

Success requires hard work and dedication. It requires perseverance. Entrepreneurs must be able to manage their resources. They must be able to utilize the right business tools. They must think of creative approaches, given both the internal and the external environment of the business.

In the middle of any challenges, an entrepreneur must be optimistic, yet practical, creative, yet action-oriented, and enthusiastic to think through the many ways to survive. Entrepreneurs must know how to keep going and learning. They recognize the importance of adaptability, resourcefulness, diligence, and commitment in their venture.

Finally, entrepreneurs must recognize that to be successful in what they do, for their micro business, they must acknowledge their present circumstances. They must embrace change if and when necessary. And they must enhance their entrepreneurial spirit to keep their drive alive.

About the Author

Sheila Atienza is a Canadian author and content creator who writes about marketing, digital media, small business and personal finance.

Some of her published works/books are available in:

University of Toronto Thomas Fisher Library; McGill University; Dalhousie University DAL Killam Library; Brown University; Library and Archives nationales du Québec; Canada Mortgage Housing Corporation; University of Lethbridge, Medicine Hat College; and other libraries across Canada and the U.S.A.

She is the author of the books: "Savings Mix: How to Manage Money and Create Strategies to Achieve Savings and Goals", "Tweets for Your Thoughts", "How to Prepare to Own a Home in Canada", and "Canadian Home Financing Simplified".

Sheila Atienza is also a marketing professional and digital media consultant based in BC, Canada.

Lightning Source UK Ltd.
Milton Keynes UK
UKHW010938200921
390891UK00001B/161